EXPLORING COUNTRIES
Madagascar

by Ellen Frazel

BELLWETHER MEDIA · MINNEAPOLIS, MN

BLASTOFF! READERS
5

Note to Librarians, Teachers, and Parents:

Blastoff! Readers are carefully developed by literacy experts and combine standards-based content with developmentally appropriate text.

Level 1 provides the most support through repetition of high-frequency words, light text, predictable sentence patterns, and strong visual support.

Level 2 offers early readers a bit more challenge through varied simple sentences, increased text load, and less repetition of high-frequency words.

Level 3 advances early-fluent readers toward fluency through increased text and concept load, less reliance on visuals, longer sentences, and more literary language.

Level 4 builds reading stamina by providing more text per page, increased use of punctuation, greater variation in sentence patterns, and increasingly challenging vocabulary.

Level 5 encourages children to move from "learning to read" to "reading to learn" by providing even more text, varied writing styles, and less familiar topics.

Whichever book is right for your reader, Blastoff! Readers are the perfect books to build confidence and encourage a love of reading that will last a lifetime!

This edition first published in 2013 by Bellwether Media, Inc.

No part of this publication may be reproduced in whole or in part without written permission of the publisher. For information regarding permission, write to Bellwether Media, Inc., Attention: Permissions Department, 5357 Penn Avenue South, Minneapolis, MN 55419.

Library of Congress Cataloging-in-Publication Data
Frazel, Ellen.
  Madagascar / by Ellen Frazel.
    p. cm. – (Blastoff! readers: Exploring countries)
  Includes bibliographical references and index.
  Summary: "Developed by literacy experts for students in grades three through seven, this book introduces young readers to the geography and culture of Madagascar"–Provided by publisher.
  ISBN 978-1-60014-861-3 (hardcover : alk. paper)
  1. Madagascar–Juvenile literature. I. Title. II. Series: Blastoff! readers. 5, Exploring countries.
  DT469.M26F73 2013
  969.1–dc23   2012029257

Printed in the United States of America, North Mankato, MN.

Contents

Madagascar is an island country off the southeastern coast of Africa. It lies in the Indian Ocean and is made up of one large island and several smaller islands. Covering 226,658 square miles (587,041 square kilometers), it is the fourth largest island in the world. In the middle of the country is Antananarivo, Madagascar's capital city.

Madagascar's closest neighbor is Mozambique to the west. The Mozambique **Channel** flows between the two countries. All major rivers in Madagascar flow into this channel.

N

W   E

S

Mozambique

Mozambique Channel

Madagascar

★
Antananarivo

Did you know?
The only islands bigger than Madagascar are Greenland, New Guinea, and Borneo.

Indian Ocean

fun fact
Madagascar has been called the "eighth continent" because of its distinct plant and animal life.

5

Madagascar is known for its unique landscapes. A steep **escarpment** on the eastern coast is home to the country's remaining **tropical rain forests**. The central part of the island is a **plateau** region. Most of the country's major cities are located on these highlands.

Did you know?

A chain of constructed waterways connects natural lakes and rivers to form the Pangalanes Canal along the eastern coast of Madagascar. This 370-mile (600-kilometer) canal is one of the longest in the world.

Pangalanes Canal

The highlands contain three major **massifs**. The country's highest point is Maromokotro, which climbs 9,436 feet (2,876 meters) on the Tsaratanana Massif. **Tropical dry forests** and **thorn forests** grow to the west and south of the central highlands. Deserts can also be found as the land slopes down in the southwest.

The Madagascar Spiny Thicket is an unusual region in the south of the country. It is a cross between a forest and a desert. Most of the plants in this region are found only in Madagascar. Some trees are tall with long, sharp spines and no branches. Baobabs and other trees have fat trunks and stubby branches. They store water in their leaves, trunks, or roots. All of these unique characteristics help the plants survive for long periods without rain.

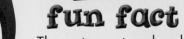

! fun fact

The octopus tree has long, spiny limbs that reach out in many directions like the arms of an octopus!

lemurs

Most of Madagascar's wildlife cannot be found anywhere else in the world. Famous for its lemurs, the island is home to around 50 **species**. The ring-tailed lemur lives in the spiny thickets and in forests along rivers.

fossa

tenrec

fun fact

Nearly half of the world's chameleon species live in Madagascar. The world's smallest chameleon was recently discovered there. It is as small as the tip of a match!

Cat-like animals called fossas chase lemurs from tree to tree. Hundreds of different butterfly species flutter among the leaves in rain forests. In tropical dry forests, tenrecs come out at night to search for worms and insects.

Over 22 million people live in Madagascar. More than 9 out of every 10 are Malagasy. About 20 different Malagasy groups live across the island. The Merina, who live mostly in the highlands, make up the largest group. Their **ancestors** came to the island hundreds of years ago from Borneo. The Betsimisaraka and Sakalava live along the coasts. Their ancestors are African, Arab, Indonesian, and Malaysian.

Small groups of Chinese, Indian, and French people also make their homes in Madagascar. The official languages of Madagascar are Malagasy, French, and English.

Speak Malagasy!

English	Malagasy	How to say it
hello	manahoana	mano-OHN
good-bye	veloma	ve-LOOM-uh
yes	eny	EH-nee
no	tsia	TZEE-uh
please	azafady	ah-zah-FAHD-ee
thank you	misaotra	mis-OW-truh
friend	namana	NAH-ma-na

Most Malagasy live as their ancestors did hundreds of years ago. About 7 out of every 10 people live in the countryside. They build houses out of mud, bamboo, or palm leaves supported by poles. Parents and children often share their homes with grandparents and other extended family. To get to the local market, people walk or take carts driven by **zebu**.

In cities, people live in houses and apartments. Some make their homes in traditional brick houses on hillsides. Roads and schools are easier to access in cities. Boats, trains, and minibuses called *taxis-brousses* take people from place to place.

Where People Live in Madagascar

cities 30%

countryside 70%

Did you know?

Women and sometimes men wear the traditional *lamba*. A *lamba* often consists of two pieces of fabric. One piece wraps around the waist or chest. The other goes around the shoulders or head.

15

Did you know?

Many children who live in the countryside cannot attend school because they must work on the farm or help raise their younger siblings. They may also live too far from school to attend every day.

School in Madagascar is free and required from ages 6 to 14. Children go to primary school for five years. They often study both Malagasy and French. They also learn basic math, reading, and writing. Children then go to secondary school for seven years. They earn a high school diploma at the end of secondary school.

Some students seek further education at the University of Antananarivo or one of several other universities in the country. They study law, medicine, and many other careers.

Did you know?

Madagascar is the world's main source of vanilla and a leading source of cloves and ylang-ylang. Oil from the ylang-ylang tree is used in many popular perfumes.

The land and sea provide many jobs for the people of Madagascar. Many fish for shrimp, shellfish, and other seafood off the coasts. Farmers grow rice in the central highlands. Coffee beans, sugarcane, and vanilla are other important crops. In the south and west, people raise zebu and other livestock. Miners dig into the earth for coal and copper. Some people work in **ports** where goods are shipped into and out of Madagascar.

Those in cities have **service jobs**. They run shops, hotels, and restaurants. Some people show **tourists** the beautiful sights of Madagascar.

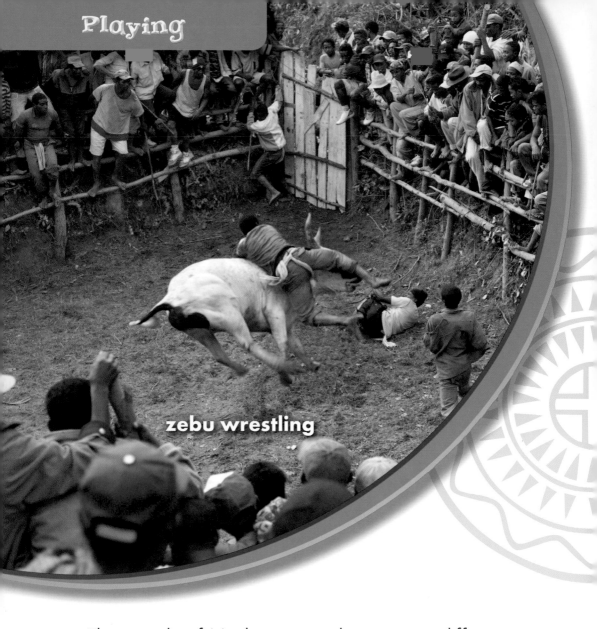

zebu wrestling

The people of Madagascar relax in many different ways. On the coasts, some practice a traditional **martial art** called *moraingy*. Two people fight with their bare hands until one person wins. In many areas, people participate in the sport of zebu wrestling. A board game called *fanorona* is popular among those in the highlands. This game is similar to checkers.

Music and storytelling are other fun activities in Madagascar. People recite poems about their Malagasy ancestors. In the highlands, traditional *Hira Gasy* performers dress in bright costumes and sing and dance for large crowds. The funky beats of *salegy* music on the coasts get people on the dance floor.

Hira Gasy

Did you know?
People love to share food in Madagascar. Someone eating even a small meal will invite a neighbor to join by calling out, "*Karibo!*"

Food brings people together in Madagascar. Families traditionally sit on a mat called a *fanambanana* to eat together. Rice is included with every meal. In the morning, families usually eat leftover rice with dried fish or small meat **kebabs**. Some enjoy doughnut-like cakes called *mokary*. They drink coffee or tea with their meal. In the afternoon, people may snack on a fritter or **samosa** from a street vendor.

Dinner is the main meal of the day. Rice is served with seafood, beans, or meat. Many families eat *kitoza*, or smoked zebu meat. A tomato sauce or a **curry** is often prepared with the rice. For dessert, people enjoy mangos, papayas, and other seasonal fruits.

fun fact

Bonbon coco is a delicious candy made from shredded coconut. It is cooked with sugar and shaped into chewy balls.

bonbon coco

samosas

Did you know?

Famadihana, or "the turning of the bones," is a Malagasy tradition. People dig up the bodies of their dead relatives, wrap them in fresh cloth, and dance with them.

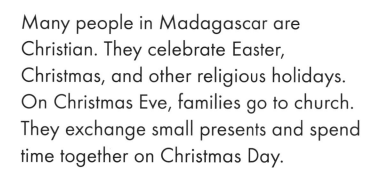

Many people in Madagascar are Christian. They celebrate Easter, Christmas, and other religious holidays. On Christmas Eve, families go to church. They exchange small presents and spend time together on Christmas Day.

Madagascar also has holidays that honor events in its history. On Memorial Day, people remember those who died fighting for Madagascar's freedom. June 26 marks the day the country gained independence from France in 1960. *Hira Gasy* performers put on a show honoring Malagasy culture. Children sing and march in the streets with colorful paper lanterns.

Independence Day

Travelers come from all over the world to see the
Avenue of the Baobabs in western Madagascar.
A group of about 20 baobabs line a dirt road there.
They tower up to 98 feet (30 meters) high, and their
trunks measure up to 36 feet (11 meters) across.

Baobabs
Amoureux

These trees were part of a dense forest hundreds of years ago. Today, people are working to preserve the Avenue of the Baobabs as well as other natural wonders of the country. Madagascar's unique plants, animals, and landscapes are a source of pride that the people hope to share with the world forever.

Fast Facts About Madagascar

Madagascar's Flag

The flag of Madagascar has one vertical white stripe on the left side. The white stands for purity. To the right are red and green horizontal bands of the same size. Red represents independence and green represents hope. This flag was adopted in 1958.

Official Name: Republic of Madagascar

Area: 226,658 square miles (587,041 square kilometers); Madagascar is the 47th largest country in the world.

Capital City:	Antananarivo
Important Cities:	Toamasina, Fianarantsoa, Mahajanga
Population:	22,005,222 (July 2012)
Official Languages:	Malagasy, French, English
National Holiday:	Independence Day (June 26)
Religions:	Traditional beliefs (52%), Christian (41%), Muslim (7%)
Major Industries:	farming, fishing, services, tourism
Natural Resources:	graphite, chromite, coal, bauxite, salt, quartz, mica, fish, hydropower
Manufactured Products:	textiles, glassware, cement, automobile parts
Farm Products:	coffee beans, vanilla, sugarcane, cloves, cocoa beans, rice, cassava, beans, bananas, peanuts, livestock
Unit of Money:	Malagasy ariary; the ariary is divided into 5 iraimbilanja.

Glossary

ancestors—relatives who lived long ago

channel—a narrow body of water between two landmasses

curry—a spicy sauce often served with rice

escarpment—a long cliff or steep slope; an escarpment usually separates two flatter areas that have different elevations.

kebabs—pieces of meat skewered on a stick and grilled

martial art—a style or technique of fighting and self-defense

massifs—the main masses of mountains or collections of mountains

plateau—an area of flat, raised land

ports—sea harbors where ships can dock

samosa—a fried pastry filled with potatoes, onions, peas, and meat

service jobs—jobs that perform tasks for people or businesses

species—groups of related animals; all animals in a species have the same characteristics.

thorn forests—areas with thick growth of thorny trees and brush found in warm, dry regions

tourists—people who travel to visit another country

tropical dry forests—forests that experience dry seasons that last for several months; tropical dry forests are not as thick as rain forests.

tropical rain forests—thick, green forests in the hot and wet regions near the equator

zebu—a type of cattle; zebu have a large hump on their shoulders.

To Learn More

AT THE LIBRARY

Kabana, Joni. *Torina's World: A Child's Life in Madagascar*. Portland, Ore.: Arnica Pub., 2007.

Oluonye, Mary N. *Madagascar*. Minneapolis, Minn.: Lerner Publications, 2010.

Powzyk, Joyce Ann. *A Little Lemur Named Mew*. Brookfield, Conn.: Millbrook Press, 2003.

ON THE WEB

Learning more about Madagascar is as easy as 1, 2, 3.

1. Go to www.factsurfer.com.

2. Enter "Madagascar" into the search box.

3. Click the "Surf" button and you will see a list of related Web sites.

With factsurfer.com, finding more information is just a click away.

Index

The images in this book are reproduced through the courtesy of: Nazzu, front cover; Hemis.fr, pp. 6-7; Pierre-Yves Babelon, p. 7, 15, 21; NHPA, p. 8; Photo Researchers/Getty Images, pp. 8-9; Minden Pictures/SuperStock, pp. 10-11; worldswildlifewonders, p. 11 (top); Eric Isselée, p. 11(middle); larus, p. 11 (bottom); R. Ian Lloyd/Masterfile, p. 12; Michel Renaudeau/Age Fotostock/SuperStock, p. 14; Christian Goupi/Age Fotostock/SuperStock, pp. 16-17, 18; Michel Renaudeau/Age Fotostock, pp. 19 (left & right), 22; Nigel Pavitt/Getty Images, p. 20; highviews, p. 23 (left); HelenaQueen, p. 23 (right); KIM LUDBROOK/EPA/Newscom, pp. 24-25; AFP/Getty Images, p. 25; Age Fotostock/SuperStock, pp. 26-27; imagebroker.net/SuperStock, p. 27; Oleg Mit, p. 29.